liminal musings

Ki Wodehouse

BookLeaf Publishing

liminal musings © 2023 Ki Wodehouse

All rights reserved.

No part of this publication may be reproduced, stored in a retrieval system, or transmitted, in any form or by any means, electronic, mechanical, photocopying, recording or otherwise, without the prior written permission of the presenters.

Ki Wodehouse asserts the moral right to be identified as author of this work.

Presentation by *BookLeaf Publishing*

Web: www.bookleafpub.com

E-mail: info@bookleafpub.com

ISBN: 9789357740517

First edition 2023

to everyone who's ever given me encouragement, i'd never be where or who i am without you

how to start

i want to be good
i want to do well
but i can't find the right words

i want to get to the end
i want to see the light
but there's so much that comes first

i want to do it all
i want to make myself proud
but i don't know how to start

i need to begin
i need to take a chance
so i'll pick up a pen and write

here we go.

daisy chain, daisy chain

daisy chain, daisy chain,
how long will this one be?
daisy chain, daisy chain,
would you pick the flowers for me?

daisy chain, daisy chain,
pick the ones with the longest stem,
daisy chain, daisy chain,
so it's easier to thread them.

daisy chain, daisy chain,
we bask in the sunshine,
daisy chain, daisy chain,
it's only here for a short time.

daisy chain, daisy chain,
your laugh's my favourite sound,
daisy chain, daisy chain,
i wish you'd stick around.

daisy chain, daisy chain,
your smile shines like gold,
daisy chain, daisy chain,
try to remember me when you're old.

daisy chain, daisy chain,
i guess that's long enough,
daisy chain, daisy chain,
it's time to grow up.

cupcakes

i'm 22, and i'm making cupcakes in my kitchen
it's been a while since i was last home,
so my family insisted.

i'm 20, and i'm making cupcakes in my kitchen
everyone seems to be baking lately,
it's a pleasant distraction.

i'm 18, and i'm making cupcakes in my kitchen
i'm thinking about my childhood,
and my future from here.

i'm 16, and i'm making cupcakes in my kitchen
i'm showing my friends how i make them,
sharing laughs as we go.

i'm 14, and i'm making cupcakes in my kitchen
i am starting to get into music,
and singing along with the door closed.

i'm 12, and i'm making cupcakes in my kitchen
i misremembered the recipe but they still taste
great,
i think i'll make them like this from now.

i'm 10, and i'm making cupcakes in my kitchen
i don't need my mum's book this time,
i remember how to do it.

i'm 8, and i'm making cupcakes in my kitchen
my mum is showing me how,
as i turn around,
and i see myself.

i'm 8,
i'm 10,
i'm 12,
i'm 14,
i'm 16,
i'm 18,
i'm 20,
i'm 22,
and i'm making cupcakes in my kitchen.

anya

i grab a pair of chopsticks
to start making pancakes
i give the batter a good mix
and hope to ease our heartache

i put on some old songs
which i think that you won't mind
i gently sing along
and hope we can unwind

in these last few days
we've said goodbye a lot
and though we'll soon part ways
right now you're all i've got

i wish we could extend
all the time that we've been sharing
so i just try to pretend
that i can't feel you staring

i know what you're doing
i've done it before too
you're taking this all in
because i'm leaving soon

normally i'd tease
normally i'd laugh
but i know how much you need
this mental photograph

so i'll sing a little louder
and make sure that you see
i'm smiling a bit bolder
to make the best memory

i'll dance a little too
as i bring you a full plate
and i'll remind you that i love you
before it is too late

it's time to go to bed
but i'll see you again tomorrow
please ignore the dread
of our coming sorrow

we'll hug away our fear
that this really is the end
our eyes are filled with tears
we truly made good friends.

everything itches

i scratch just below my eye
itch, itch, itch
tears want to escape
but i can't let them.

i scratch just below my lips
itch, itch, itch
words want to escape
but i can't let them.

i scratch just below my neck
itch, itch, itch
sighs want to escape
but i can't let them.

i scratch just below my chest
itch, itch, itch
my feelings want to escape,
but i can't let them.

my soul wants to escape
and leak out through my skin
i can't scratch this one back in place
it's almost at the surface now.

watch me disappear with it.

short sleeves

fingertips grace my forearm and all the nerves
light up
will they ever get used to this softer kind of
touch?
they're admiring my tattoo and i pretend that i
don't care
i just pray that they don't see why it's really
there.

bad brain day

my mind feels a little heavier today
it's hard to get out of bed
i didn't sleep too well last night
and i can feel it in my head

get out of bed, go to the bathroom
use the toilet and brush my teeth
don't forget to take your tablets
or the heaviness will just increase

i missed my class, i even prepared for it
i'll just have to apologise next week
i think i'll do some housekeeping instead
but i just feel so weak

open my laptop, check my email
there's nothing that needs to be done
i'll sit in my room and fail to notice
the setting of the sun

in the dark, i still can't see
this light i want to follow
have a shower and attempt to sleep
i'll try again tomorrow.

sky

you've only just been born from light
and you're not sure what to do
you call out for any attention
and i can tell you're new

let me light your candle, little moth
i'll show you the way around
i'll show you all my favourite places
and all the secrets to be found

i'll show you the best ways to travel
and how to befriend these creatures
i'll help you with your daily tasks
and you can change your features

i think we both should have a rest now
we've been exploring for quite long
maybe we'll sit for a little while
and i'll play you a song

and the end of it all, a big white candle
i say thank you with a high five
it's time to go, little moth, but i'll see you again
next time we're both online

entity

there's an entity that follows me
he's quite the combination
of all those who remind me
of my griefs and my regrets.

there's an entity that follows me
i open doors for him
he takes the corner of every room
and watches me with care.

there's an entity that follows me
even in my quietest moments
he hears my thoughts and feels my soul
more than any real person could know.

there's an entity that follows me
a creation of my own
i preform for him who i feel i should be
and try to hide the parts i hate.

there's an entity that follows me
for how long i couldn't say
i hate to think i could be alone
with only myself some day.

there's an entity that follows me
i wish he were really there
he's the consequence of feeling alone
and deeply misunderstood.

there's an entity that follows me
he knows me all too well
when i sense him in his corner
i feel understood.

there's an entity that follows me
i'd hate if he were real
for if i were to meet these people again
they'd know me all too well.

misplaced

name
i don't know what my name is
but i know which one to say
it's just a sound i have to react to
when someone wants my attention
it's not me.

face
i don't know how my face looks
but i know which one people see
it's just the thing i look at in the mirror
and try to make look nice
it's not me.

clothes
i don't know what clothes suit me
but i know what's in my closet
it's just something to wrap myself in
for practicality and comfort
it's not me.

home
i don't know where my home is
but i know where i live
it's just a place where i can sleep
and store all of my things
it's not me.

mask
i don't know how i act
but i know which mask to wear
it's just some basic scripts
that real people use
it's not me.

soul
i don't know if i belong here
but i know it's where i am
it's just the life i have to live
and hope it wasn't meant for someone else
is this me?

community

i'm in a room full of people,
we all get along really well,
i'm not friends with everyone here,
but it's one big community.

i've been here before,
and i'll be here again,
but every time it's different,
different room, different people.

soon enough, like always,
when we've all parted ways,
their faces will blur together,
and i'll forget all of their names.

and i hate it.

i love these people, i really do
we all get along so well;
we've laughed,
danced,
sung,
cooked,
watched movies,
played games,

even climbed mountains,
and swam in the sea,
lived and loved and learned,
all together.

how can i leave this room knowing
that it'll all become nothing more
than a faded memory?

limbo

everything is heavy

my mind, body, soul

i move in slow motion

every action is taken with great caution and care

but without a single thought

my joints crack

there isn't enough space in my lungs for the air i
need

and my hands are ever so slightly numb

and light

my ulcer bites at my mouth should i try to eat

and won't even let me spit out a single word

i try to silence it with salt

but it doubles in size

i don't know if i'm hungry or nauseous

my head spins

but i will not faint

a sudden ache in my chest traps me in place

and then

i move on.

perhaps i am unwell.

body

i have freckles that corner my lips
and make it look like i have snake bites

i have a tattoo on my forearm
of a 6-flowered daisy chain

i have strawberry blond hair
that i wear the same way every day

i have a scar on my stomach
from when i fell out of a tree when i was 12

i have a freckle on my forearm
i always thought looked like a car

i have rosy red cheeks
that can still somehow blush even brighter

i have scars down my forearm
you only see if you know they exist

it's all me, it's all mine,
but somehow my soul doesn't fit quite right

i'm still trying to figure out
how to make this house feel like a home

despair / truth

how do you let
your emotions flow so freely?

how do you let
your soul pass through your lips?

how do you let
your smile break my heart?

how do you let
your eyes fill with tears?

how do you let
your face shine with pride?

how do you let
your blood stain my shirt?

how do you let
me beg you not to do this?

how do you let
your love for me come out?

how do you let
yourself say goodbye?

and how do you let
it take you away
before i can figure out how to say it back?

neither

it's finally playtime! horray!
i don't know what i want to do...
i think that maybe today,
i'll try something new!

i see the boys playing football,
and it looks like lots of fun!
i can't play it at all...
but i could learn from someone!

i approach them all to see,
if they'll let me join in...
they smile wide with glee,
"of course, let's begin!"

they grab a small stack of chairs,
for me to sit on like a throne!
they explain the game while i sit and stare,
i don't have to learn on my own!

now the rules are understood,
i can finally have a try!
i actually think i'm doing good!
feeling just like another guy...

i'm glad i got to have a go,
the boys were all suprised...
but now i'm running with them to and fro,
feeling slightly more disguised.

time's up, miss is ringing the bell,
playtime has to end...
a small crack's appeared in my shell,
should i join their game again?

i lie in bed that night,
trying to figure out how i feel...
they were so full of shock and delight,
was it that big a deal?

does it really matter what i do,
just because i'm a "girl"?
i really don't have a clue,
and it's making my brain whirl...

being a girl makes my heart ache...
but i don't want to be a boy either.
i really wish with all it takes,
that it's possible to be neither.

god

the sound of a waterfall
the hug of a friend
the sky at sunrise
the crashing of waves
the laughter of a child
the blooming of a flower
the strum of a guitar
the early spring breeze
the moon and her stars
the concept of art
the roots of a tree
the northern lights
the top of a mountain
the song of a wood pigeon
the shape of a river
the lamppost at the end of the road

googly eyes

"i really hate that you have to carry that around
for me" she apologises
"i don't mind at all," i reply, doing my best to
reassure her, "as long as you let me put googly
eyes on it"
she gives a light hearted sigh and continues
walking. making jokes has often been the easiest
way for me to get through to people when i don't
know how.

i set the chair down for her again, a quick little
pit stop.
this is a good opportunity for me to run into the
nearby primark for a fresh set of pyjamas for
her.
i tell them both "i won't be long!" and run inside.
it doesn't take me long to grab some pyjamas
and pay for them.

the shop's exit is on the other side of the building
to the entrance, so now i have to circle back
around.
that's fine, i get to walk back through this street
with rainbow umbrellas hanging overhead
and along that street... well that's just perfect!

i head straight into the works, eyes scanning for
their stickers
i find them tucked away in the back corner, and
sitting right there-
a pack of ten for only £1!? well now i just have
to get them!

i finally make it back to the two of them, and
explain that the exit was on the other side
i pull the pyjamas out the bag so she can have a
look, she seems to like them.
"and..." i say, "i got these!" as i pull the giant
googly eyes out with a flourish. maybe i wasn't
joking after all.

i'm met with a chuckle and an eye roll, but
before anyone can refuse i'm already ripping
open the bag.
i pull two out and stick them evenly on the back
of her chair, trying not to giggle like a complete
child.
"there we are, perfect!" i say to a couple smiles,
one genuine and one slightly irritated.

back at the hotel i start to think, what can i use
these other googly eyes for?
and i realise now's my chance to use a couple
more on the front of the chair...
i do it before anyone can realise, and now he has
a friendly face from both sides!

we all find it funny now, and take a couple
photos to share online
well, now we have to think of a name for him!
we have a few ideas, i can't remember them all
now, but one just seemed to stick.

she's not around anymore, and we all miss her a
lot.
it's been hard to turn her home back into a house.
we're all surrounded by her things, and it's very
bittersweet.

now, when i see pedro, the googly-eyed chair,
stored in the basement or sat in the dining room
i think about her, everything she did for us,
every joke we shared. and i think about that trip
i reminisce, and i smile, and i try not to think
about the end. and then i walk away, back to
whatever i was doing before.

neither ii

i think about that a lot

i usually frame it as a joke

but i used to hate myself for it

i wished i could go back in time

slap that poor child in the face

grab them by the shoulders and scream

"it IS possible to be neither!! you ARE neither!!"

maybe i'd scream

"the quicker you accept that

and the quicker you voice it

the easier your life will be!"

and maybe that child would be shocked

and maybe they would cry

maybe they wouldn't even understand

but these days i wish i were softer to myself

now i wish i could go back in time

give that poor child a hug

embrace them by the shoulders and whisper

"it's okay. it'll all be okay."

maybe i'd say

"you'll figure it out in time

and there are people who will understand you

and you can always change your mind."

maybe then i'd chuckle,

"goodness knows i have."

and maybe that child would be reassured

they'd probably still cry

all they needed was a listening ear

and for someone to treat them softly

they'll figure it out soon enough

when they finally learn the right words

before then they'll have many more thoughts

that they'll look back on with a laugh

"it was so obvious!" they'll think

"how did i not realise sooner!"

they'll think knowing earlier would make
everything easier

as if coming out is a one-time thing

and not something i still have to frequently face

but that's okay, they'll learn, in time

just as i did

that they should treat themself more softly

and how to fall in love with their shadow

if everything went my way

if everything went my way,
i like to sit and ponder,
what an interesting life it would be...

i'd be at a different uni,
well, i'd have graduated by now,
with a slightly different degree

i'd still be in contact with my childhood best
friend,
maybe i'd be in a long-term relationship,
and i'd get on better with my family.

i'd understand my identity,
everyone would use the right words for me,
and maybe my body would fit a bit better.

i'd have spent more time on my hobbies,
and even published a thing or two,
maybe it'd get a little bit of attention.

everything would be great,
i'd have no reason to be sad,
but i wonder if i'd feel something missing.

you see, if everything went my way,
there's so many opportunities i'd never have
gotten,
and so many things i'd never have done.

if i had everything i wanted, there's one big
problem,
asides from all the lessons i never would have
learned,
well, my dear, i never would have met you.

if everything went my way,
i don't think i'd be as fulfilled.
so, maybe i am lucky after all.

time

time is moving ever so slowly
life is going on for so long
it feels like it's been forever
but it's barely begun

how can i pass all this time
what am i supposed to do
i can see so far ahead
but it's all so blurry

time moves so fast
life is going too quickly
it feels like i need a rest
but i have things to do tomorrow

how can i do everything
what am i supposed to chose
i can barely see past this week
but i can feel the deadlines looming

spring

this winter was quite rough

it's honestly a miracle i made it through

now the season's finally ending

i'm waiting for the clouds to part again

flowers are starting to peek out

the summer sun will arrive before long

they say spring starts on a specific date

but for me it's always some time in february

when the spring sun first breaks from the clouds

its gentle warmth holds my face

i close my eyes

and bask in it like a cat

the spring sun cleanses the air

and brings me a soft breeze

i breathe it all in

it fills me completely

it rinses all my organs

it blows away the winter's cobwebs

and i feel my hope renewed

shining through like a star in the dark

and i know the sun will rise again